When Papaw Went to Heaven

Leah Harris
Illustrations by Blueberry Illustrations

Copyright © 2021 by Leah Harris

All rights reserved.
No part of this book may be reproduced
or transmitted in any form or by any means
without written permission from the author.

ISBN-979-8-9853972-0-8

In loving memory of my dad (*our Papaw*), David Stanley Starr. May your memory always live on within my children's hearts and may your legacy be remembered. I love you, Daddy.

Papaw and I had a special relationship.

I have so many memories of us together.

When I was born, Papaw was one of the first people to hold me.

In Papaw's arms, I was safe and warm.

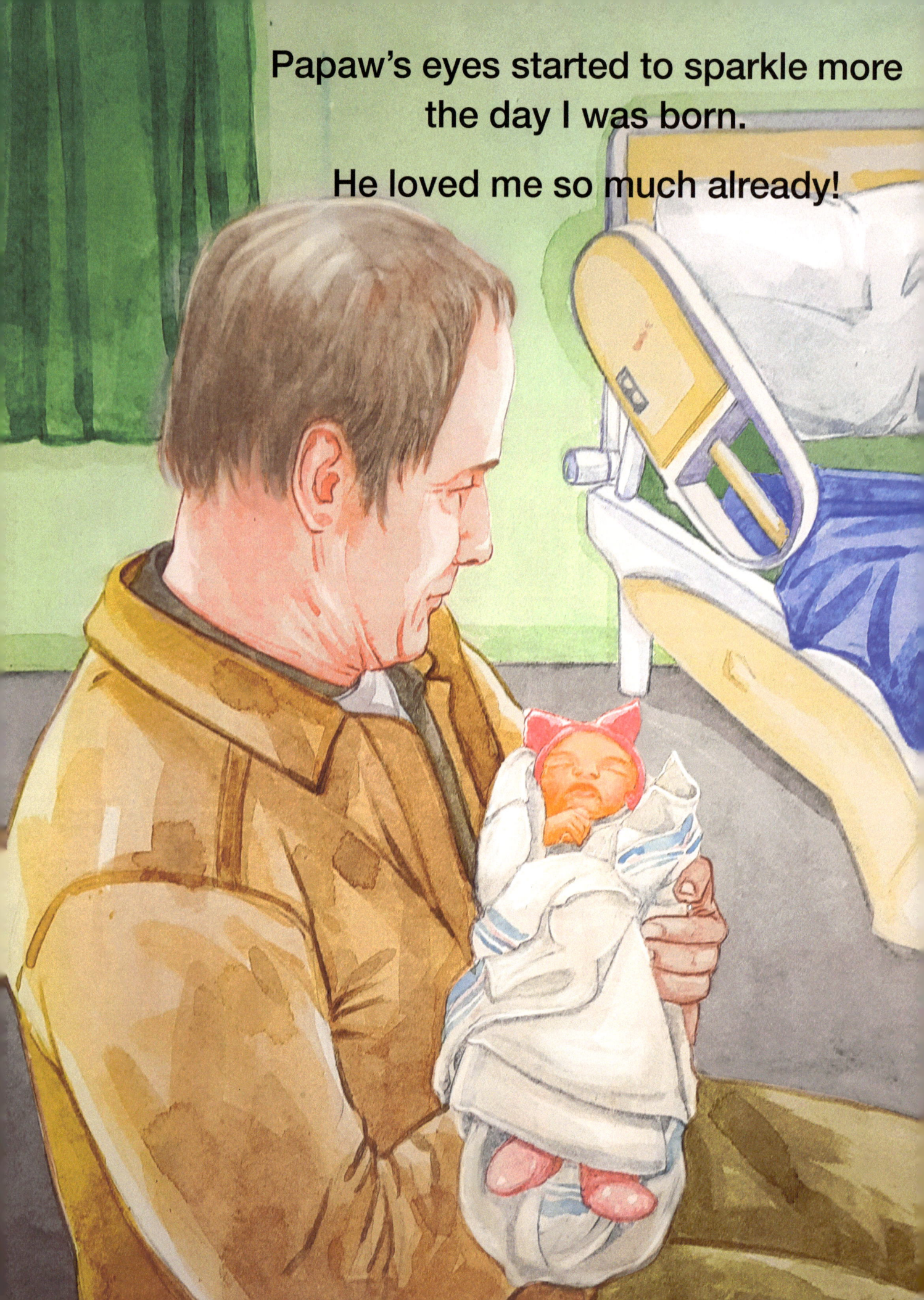

When I was a little baby, Papaw loved holding me and watching me grow.

As I grew up, Papaw and I spent a lot of time together.

Papaw, Mommy, Daddy, and I would go on wild adventures.

We would drive to the safari park where there were many different kinds of animals.

We saw llamas, zebras, monkeys, tortoises, wallabies, and kangaroos too!

Papaw especially liked the llamas.

We would feed the animals from our car. It was so much fun!

I also really loved going to Papaw's house.

There were so many deer in Papaw's backyard!

Daddy and I would go outside to see them and would count all of the deer.
Then we would come back and tell Mommy and Papaw all that we saw.

"Mommy deer, Daddy deer, and baby deer," I reported.
"Oh, how did you know it was a Daddy deer?" Mommy asked.

Papaw loved to spend time with me in other ways too.

He would help me read my favorite books while I sat in his lap.

When my baby brother was born, Papaw was so proud of me for being a great big sister and for helping Mommy.

Papaw's eyes began to sparkle even more when he met my little brother!

One day, it got very cold where we lived and there was a very bad ice storm.

We could not go outside for very long and we could not go see Papaw!

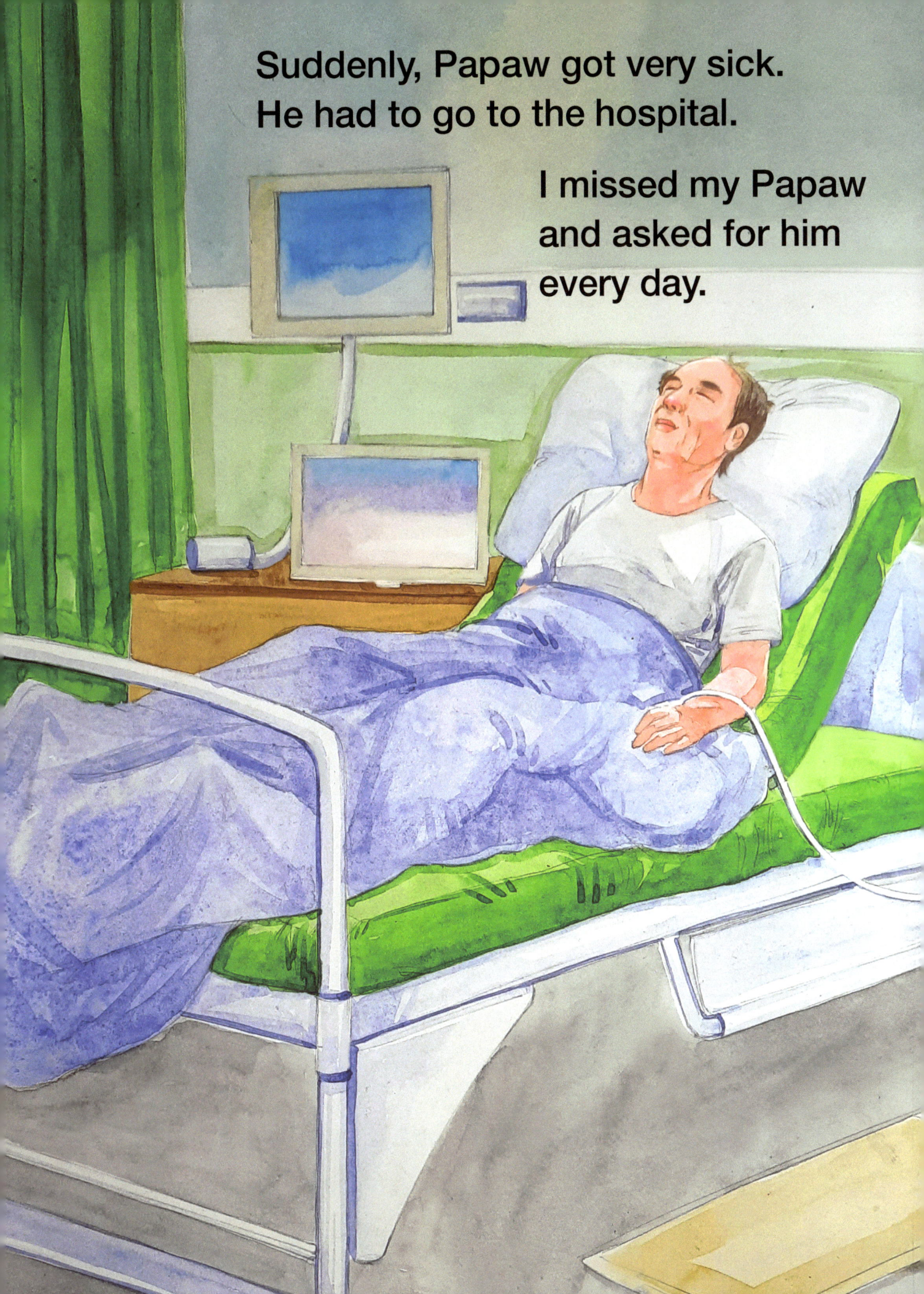

Sadly, I did not get to spend time with my Papaw anymore.

Mommy was gone a lot to be with him.

"Papaw sick?" I asked Mommy over the phone. "Mommy help Papaw?"

"Yes, baby. Mommy and the doctors are trying to get him better," Mommy answered.

Every morning, I prayed with Daddy for Papaw's healing.

I really missed my Papaw and wanted to see him again.

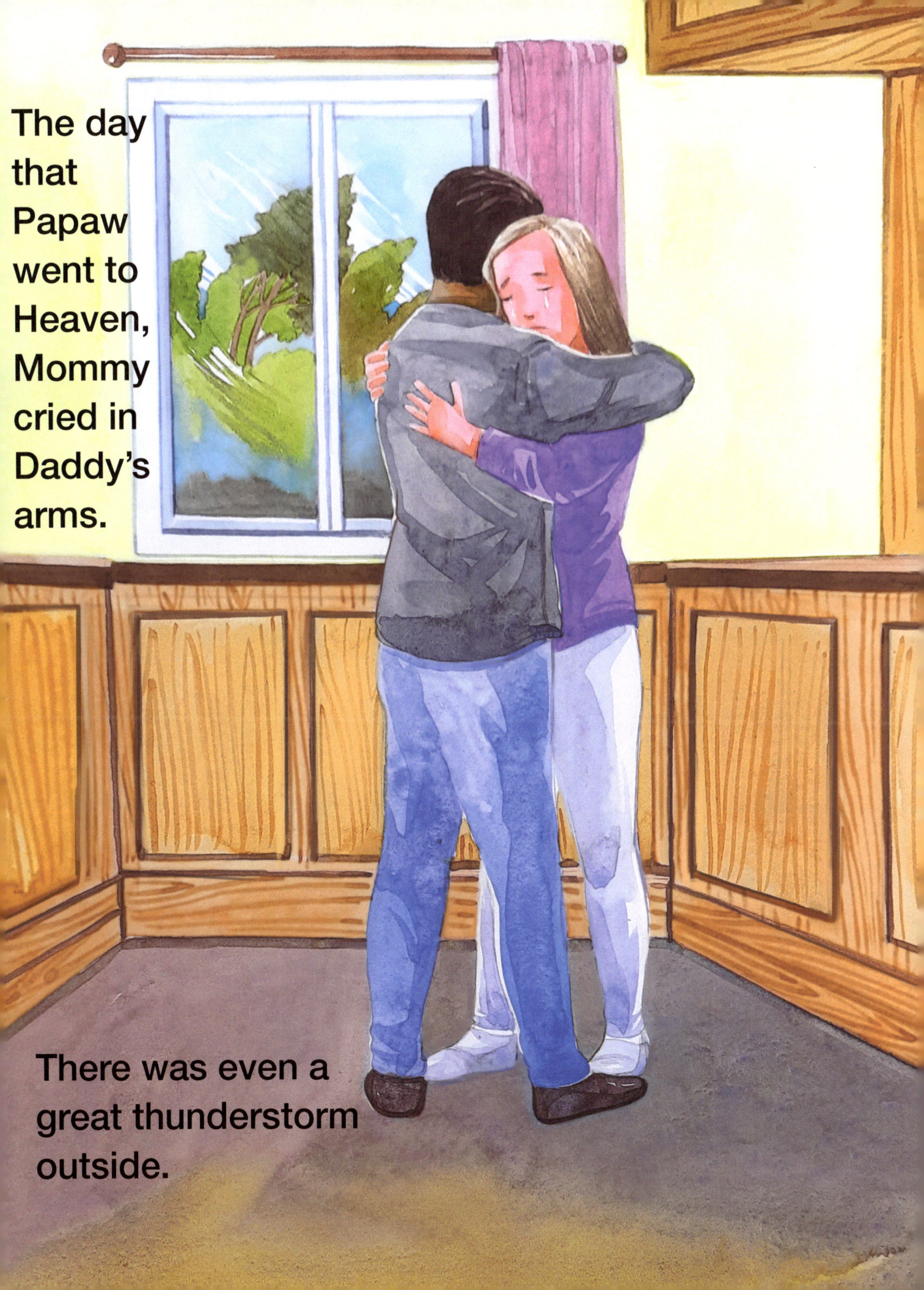

The day that Papaw went to Heaven, Mommy cried in Daddy's arms.

There was even a great thunderstorm outside.

After Papaw went to Heaven, I thought about Papaw a lot.

"Papaw sick?" I asked Mommy.

"No, baby. Papaw is not sick anymore. He is better."

"Papaw went to Heaven," Mommy replied.

"Papaw happy?" I asked.

"Yes, baby. He is happy," Mommy assured me.

"Papaw jumping?" I questioned.

"Yes, honey. Papaw is jumping and running around in Heaven. He is feeling much better and is very happy," Mommy said.

"We won't see Papaw for a while. And it's okay to be sad or for us to miss him."

"But we will see him again in Heaven. Always remember that."

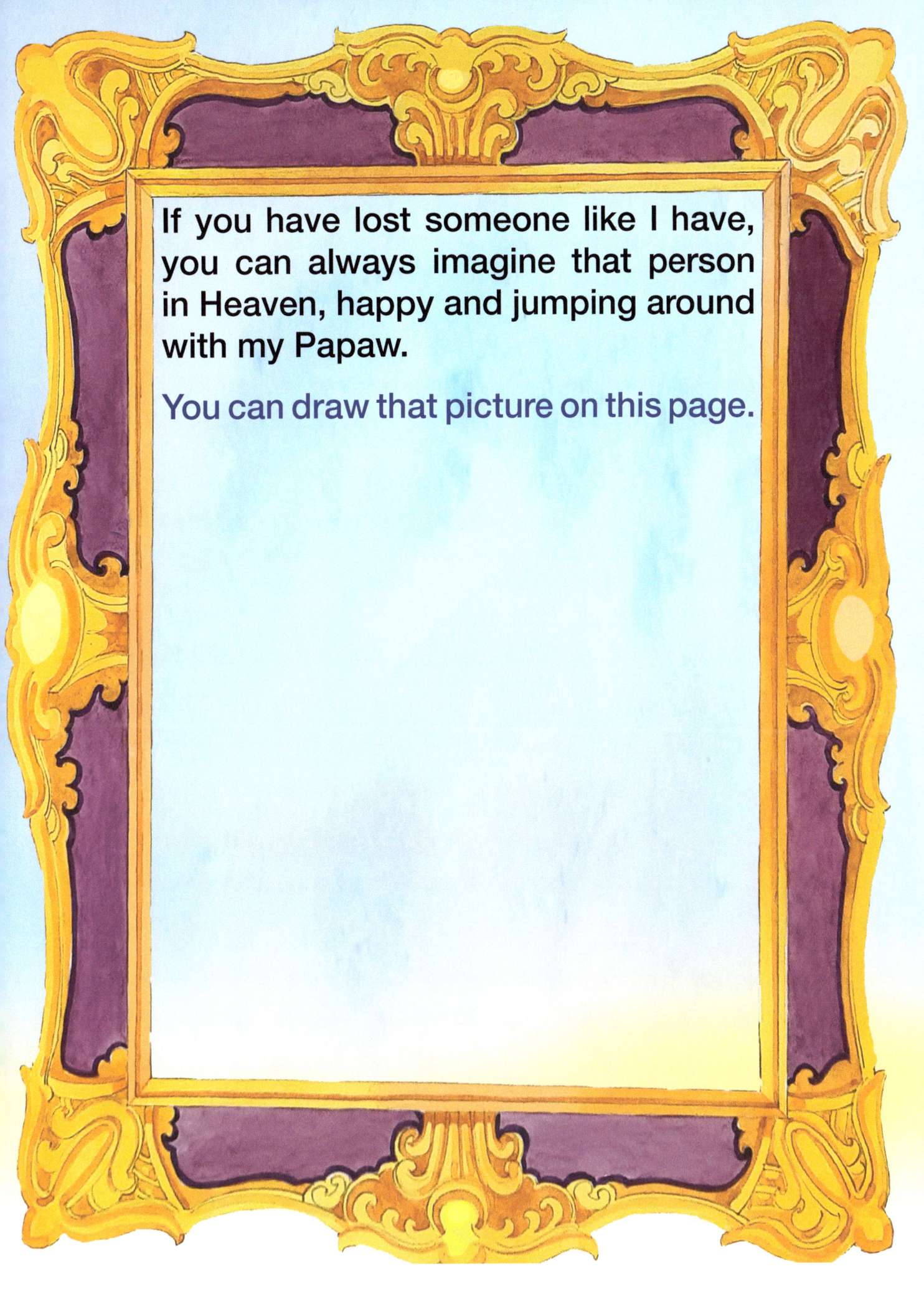

If you have lost someone like I have, you can always imagine that person in Heaven, happy and jumping around with my Papaw.

You can draw that picture on this page.

Therapeutic Activities and Resources to Help Children Process Through Grief

The following are a few recommended activities and resources to help children process the loss of a pet, friend, or family member. These may be easily modified to suit individual needs and circumstances.

Memory Box: The concept of a memory box is to create a special box, which could be a shoe box, a small wooden box, a handmade box, or anything of the like! The outside of the box can be decorated however the child pleases, whether it be painted, drawn, decorated with stickers, or words that remind the child of the special someone lost. The inside of the memory box will become a home to any personal belongings or sentimental objects that remind the child of this special someone. Some examples include a photograph, a drawn picture or poem, and/or the person's belongings such as a leash or watch. The idea behind making a memory box is that the process itself is healing and the child also has access to this special box when especially missing his or her loved one.

Grief Narrative: When Papaw Went to Heaven is an example of a grief narrative. The author has put together special memories between her dad and her daughter to help preserve these memories for years to come. This is something older children can do with help or alone, depending on the child's preference. It is also something a parent or guardian can create on behalf of small children while involving the child as is appropriate for the child's developmental level. Writing down stories and memories in a journal of that special someone is a healing journey with a lot of power in it! This activity can even take the shape of a story book with a couple of pieces of paper folded in half and stapled together on which the child can draw a picture of the memory described on each page.

Picture Album: Helping a child put together a photo album of the special someone who is dearly missed is a very therapeutic way to help the child process through grief. Picking out stickers and drawing pictures for children who love to be creative is a great way to spark the child's imagination and help engage them therapeutically for years to come.

Securing Special Moments: Being able to secure special moments is a hodge-podge of all the aforementioned therapeutic activities. The goal is to store all of the treasured items in an easily accessible area that keeps them safe. An idea that may work well is to have a chest in which the child is able to keep all the special belongings related to the grief process that can be stored away for safekeeping but pulled out easily as needed.

These activities can be easily facilitated by parents or guardians.

Recommended Resources for Children Processing Through Grief

The Invisible String by Patrice Karst

When Dinosaurs Die by Laurie Krasny Brown

The Memory Box: A Book About Grief by Joanna Rowland

Leah Harris  is a Licensed Professional Counselor (LPC) in the State of Texas who has enjoyed working with children for many years. She loves exploring the worlds of children through creative means and has two beautiful children of her own. Her husband, Sterling Harris, is very supportive of her many imaginative adventures, including singing and songwriting, writing children's books and devotionals, and pursuing a doctorate in Counselor's Education and Supervision at Liberty University. You can learn more about their ministry at SterlingHarris.org.

www.ingramcontent.com/pod-product-compliance
Lightning Source LLC
Chambersburg PA
CBHW040725060526
44119CB00083B/329